THE SHAWL and PRAIRIE DU CHIEN

OTHER PLAYS BY DAVID MAMET
Published by Grove Press

American Buffalo
Edmond
Glengarry Glen Ross
Goldberg Street: Short Plays and Monologues
Lakeboat
A Life in the Theatre
Reunion and *Dark Pony*
Sexual Pervisity in Chicago and *The Duck Variations*
The Water Engine and *Mr. Happiness*
The Woods

THE SHAWL and PRAIRIE DU CHIEN

Two Plays by David Mamet

Grove Press, Inc./New York

First Grove Press Edition 1985
First Evergreen Edition 1985

Library of Congress Cataloging-in-Publication Data

Mamet, David
     The shawl: and, Prairie du Chien.

     I. Mamet, David. Prairie du Chien. 1985. II. Title.
III. Title: Prairie du chien.
PS3563.A4345S5 1985   812'.54   85-14884
ISBN 0-8021-5172-8

For performance of such songs mentioned in *Prairie du Chien* as are in copyright, the permission of the copyright owners must be obtained; or other songs in the public domain substituted.

For the sound effects specified in *Prairie du Chien*, contact Thomas J. Valentino Inc., 151 West 46th Street, New York, NY 10036 for record no. 5008—Train Sounds.

Book design by David Miller

Printed in the United States of America

Grove Press
841 Broadway
New York, NY 10003

97 98 99 00 10 9 8 7 6 5 4 3 2

THE SHAWL and
PRAIRIE DU CHIEN

The Shawl

The Shawl was first presented on April 19, 1985, by the Goodman Theatre's New Theatre Company in Chicago as the premiere production of their Briar Street Theatre, with the following cast:

John	*Mike Nussbaum*
Miss A	*Lindsay Crouse*
Charles	*Gary Cole*

Directed by GREGORY MOSHER

THE CHARACTERS

John	A man in his fifties
Miss A	A woman in her late thirties
Charles	A man in his thirties

THE SCENE

John's office

Act One

John and Miss A

John: . . . You see:

Miss A: I don't know . . .

John: Well, there is a rhythm in our lives, and at each point, at each point each of us should be doing that thing which corresponds to this rhythm. (*Pause.*) When you awaken it is to be brusque, to . . . to be hungry (*pause*), to cleanse your mind for new impressions. (*Pause.*) To be acquisitive. At night it is appropriate to *think*, to meditate. And so it is with your life. (*Pause.*) You have a problem. What does this mean? In your life, in your day, in your . . . as each one has his rhythm . . . you . . . and so *you* do. For we look at the stars. As they did. What do we see? We see this: that they named the constellations on their knowledge of the traits which appear in that . . .

Miss A: In . . . ?

John: In that period. You see? It was the *period* that they observed. How the *moon* . . . (*Pause.*) How the *moon*, for example . . . *influences* us. Influences *planting, reaping.* How in *our* lives we are influenced. At one time in your life. At most times, perhaps, you would, you would not be here. Would you? (*Pause.*)

Miss A: No.

John: No. Of course not. So we say, what is it that troubles you? And that you probably desire that I *inform* you. Is this not so?

(*Pause.*)

Yes?

Miss A: I don't understand.

John: I think you do. You've come to me for help. You wish me to resolve your "problem." First, though, you would like me to inform you what that problem is.

Miss A: I . . .

John: Is that not correct — to surmise . . . it's alright. . . . to "guess" . . . you want me to exhibit my *power.* Is this not the truth? Is this not so? It is so. You wish me to, in effect, "read your mind." (*Pause.*) For the question is: WHAT POWERS EXIST? And what powers DO exist? And what looks after us? And . . . do you see? This is a rational concern. *Is* there an order in the world. And . . . you ask . . . and *can* things be known. *Can* things be known. (*Pause.*) And, of course, they *can*.

Miss A: . . . they can.

John: Of *course* they can, as you have suspected. (*Pause.*) Have you not?

Miss A: Have I suspected it . . . ?

John: Yes. And you have. For I see that *you* have . . . *you* have some psychic ability.

Miss A: I do . . .

John: And you have *felt* it. Yes. You have. Questioned it. But felt it. Said it was . . . *Answer* me, now . . . You said it was . . . you said it was . . . ? Have one moment's faith. Answer me. You said it was . . . ?

Miss A: Coincidence.

John: Exactly. But it was not. When you felt it. In

those instances you know that I refer to. And you know the power of which I speak. (*Pause.*) *Don't* you. (*Pause.*) *Don't* you?

Miss A: Yes.

John: I know you do. And it *is* real. As we know it is real. And why should we be frightened? To *know* . . . ? And it is *better* to know. (*Pause.*) For we say "knowledge," what is it? It is our attempt to be part of something which continues. Which we *are* part of. And *fear* — what is it? We fear that thing that we wish does not exist. But we know it exists. Don't we? (*Pause.*)

Miss A: I don't know.

John: Yes, you *do*. For what has brought you here? That knowledge. That there is a hidden order in the world. And once you dreamed this. You . . . you sat and dreamed this meeting with me. Long ago.

Miss A: I did . . .

John: *Dreamed* this when you were young . . . isn't that so? Isn't that so — *long* ago. Dreamt that you would one day sit with me. Didn't you? (*Pause.*)

Miss A: Yes.

John: I know that you did. In summer. When you were a little girl. Late summer. Sitting on a — what is it? By . . . is it by the *water* . . . ?

Miss A: Yes.

John: It *is*. Where is this?

Miss A: At . . .

John: At your home. Is it not? At your summer . . .

Miss A (*simultaneously with "summer"*): Yes. Our summer home.

John: I see . . . you by a tree. An oak? You sat and dreamed this meeting.

Miss A: Yes.

John: And I see another time of psychic power. When, you might have said "suspicion" . . . A suspicion warned you of catastrophe. Is that correct?

(*Pause.*)

Miss A: Yes.

John: I see that it is. And you were right, is this not . . . ?

Miss A: Yes. I was.

John: And I see *other* danger . . . and I see . . . (*Pause.*) When you were *young. Blood.* When you were *quite* young. A fall. And you bear the scar still. Twice in your life you have been near death. Once that you knew of, once that you did not. Now think of the times I am speaking of. (*Pause.*) Danger. When you were in grave danger. And you will *remember* what I mean, no, there is nothing to be frightened of. What is it? Please?

Miss A: You said "a scar."

John: That is correct. That is another time. A fall. But now: think back to . . . a time of physical danger.

Miss A: A . . . I don't . . . (*Pause.*)

John: Yes? (*Pause.*) What?

Miss A: Where is this scar?

John: It is on your left knee. What is it? (*Pause.*)

Miss A: Oh . . .

John: Yes?

Miss A: I don't have a scar there. (*Pause.*)

John: You are quite wrong. And I see that you have forgotten it. As it is small. Now: if you would — if you would . . . if you would look now you'll see that scar. Would you like me to turn away?

Miss A: I don't.

John (*simultaneously with "don't"*): It's alright. As I see it's important to you. You want to say you don't mean to "test" me . . . But you must trust me. And I am going to turn away. You look, and you'll see the scar.

Miss A: It's alright. I don't have to see the . . . I *believe* . . .

John (*simultaneously with "believe"*): No. You *must* look. *Not* belief but truth. Truth. For it is there. And that answers your doubts.

Miss A: I don't have a scar there.

John: Then you will prove me wrong, and then you'll know. Isn't it better to know? (*Pause.*) A small scar on your left . . .

Miss A: Oh.

John: I'm sorry? (*Pause.*) I'm sorry.

Miss A: I don't. I don't know what to say.

John: . . . what to say . . . Tell me what you saw.

Miss A: There is a scar. I have a scar on my knee.

John: Yes.

Miss A: I never knew it was there.

John (*simultaneously with "was"*): Yes. A small scar. You were quite young. When you were small then it was large. And it was traumatic, and so you repress it. We repress so much. But it all casts its shadow, and the things which you would know are all in you and all . . . *available* to you. (*Pause.*) Now: I see a loss. And I see suffering in your life. I see a loss. I . . . either you or someone close to you has suffered a tragedy.

Miss A (*softly*): Yes.

John: Please . . . ?

Miss A: Yes.

John: Recently.

Miss A: Yes. The loss of my . . .

John: Of your mother. Yes. (*Pause.*)

Miss A: You see that?

John: Wait a moment, now . . .

Miss A: I . . . you *see* that . . . ?

John: Please. Try to . . . just . . . try to relax your . . .

Miss A (*simultaneously with "your"*): My *mother.*

John: I know that you loved her very much. Don't

• 11

speak. And I see, *further* . . . (*Pause.*) I see . . . we were speaking: of that time in summer. We were speaking. She was near you then. No. She was *in* the house. You. You sat by the water. That time that you *dreamed* this. She was nearby. It's alright. I promise you. You are safe now, no harm can come to you here. She was *near* to you that time that you dreamed this meeting.

Miss A: Yes.

John: And she came out and she smiled. Now (Miss A *starts to cry.*) it's alright. (*Pause.*) It's alright. It's *good*. For you *must* mourn her . . . For she is very much with us now.

Miss A: My . . .

John: Yes.

Miss A: My *mother* . . . you *see* her?

John: I see her as she was, I sense her *through* you. Your . . . images . . . feelings . . . I see that *time* . . .

Miss A: What does she look like?

John (*simultaneously with "like"*): And I see a question in your mind. Which you will not phrase, and that question is — listen to me for I am going to answer it; that question is this — and you must not feel foolish; that question is: (*pause*) can one contact her? Can she be contacted. (*Pause.*) Although that is not the thing that has brought you here. But it arises. Can one raise the dead. (*Pause.*) Now; do you wish to know that? (*Pause.*) Answer me.

Miss A: Yes.

John: Yes. I know. For I see how many times in the day you have thought of her. *Longed* for her . . . Moments in *childhood* which have returned . . . loneliness . . . (*Pause.*) In your deep grief. And the questions of the spirit rise. And troubled, you come here. And we will *lift* your troubles. And answer your doubts. As all is open. (*Pause.*) I would like you to come back tomorrow. And bring me a photograph of her. And now (for the time is not right for that *other* question) let us address that which brings you here today. In the midst of your grief. Where everything . . . where so much, as we see, is pain. And I see you've had *much* sorrow in your life. And yet . . . and I see strength . . . and you have borne through it.

Miss A: I have . . .

John (*simultaneously with "I"*): You were going to say "you have attempted to," but you *have* . . . and you have survived. Your father . . .

Miss A: Died when I was . . .

John: And now you bear up beneath this double burden. And an active trouble comes to you. A *question* rises. Which has led you here. (*Pause.*) It concerns money. Is this not . . . ? (*Pause.*) Is this not?

Miss A: Yes. How do you know?

John (*simultaneously with "know"*): And I see a matter of the law. A legal . . .

Miss A: My . . .

John: It is your mother's will.

Miss A: Oh, my god.

John: Is this not . . . ? (*Pause.*)

Miss A: Yes.

John: And you have come to *ask* me. If you should contest the will.

Miss A: How do you know that?

John: I . . . (*Pause.*) I . . . (*Pause.*) You must . . . (*Pause.*) Let us continue:

Act Two

Charles and John

Charles: She came in.

John: . . . More tea?

Charles: Thank you.

John: Quite good don't you think?

Charles: Mmm

John: Scald the pot.

Charles: As you say . . .

John: Yes. She came in.

Charles: And — (*Pause.*) You said she wasn't married.

John: Why? Why did I say that?

Charles: Because . . . she had no ring.

John: She *had* no ring. But, no, that isn't why I said it. You see: it comes down to confidence. They'll *test* you. And you can do nothing till you have their trust.

You watch their eyes . . . I mentioned the word "husband" . . . and her eyes did nothing. So we *confirm* she isn't married. Always confirm. (*Pause.*) They want to confess. Their question is: can They Confess to *You*? Can They Trust You. (*Pause.*) A woman. Comes to you . . . she's troubled . . . for why would they come if they were not? (*Pause.*) Eh?

Charles: They wouldn't.

John: No. So what do I do? What could trouble one? Anxiety. Or worry. Loss. And so I said, "A tragedy."

Charles: You said, "to you or someone close to you."

John: As who has not. You, you see? Seeming divination. Only common sense, and the idea of the *mystic* frees her to expound. Is this worth money? (*Pause.*)

Charles: On which subject.

What do you have left?

John: What?

Charles: How much do you have left?

John: Of? (*Pause.*)

Charles: Of the fifty.

John: Of the fifty she gave me?

Charles: Yes.

John: I have all of it left.

Charles: . . . you . . . ?

John: Yes?

Charles: You have it all left?

John: Yes.

Charles: How did you buy the tea?

John: Smiled at the Grocer's Boy. (*Pause*.) I opened an account.

Charles: . . . you . . . ?

John: Went down . . . on the strength of our new friend. I opened an account.

Charles: And they let you?

John: Yes.

Charles: You didn't spend the fifty.

John (*simultaneously with "fifty"*): How could I? The bill is for "confidence."

Charles: For confidence.

John: Yes. And I have to give it back to her tomorrow. She signed her name on it. You . . . I'd . . . I'd give it to you. But . . .

Charles: . . . I didn't ask you for it . . .

John: . . . but I have to give it back to her tomorrow. The same bill . . . What did I say?

Charles: . . . you. I heard what you said.

John (*simultaneously with "said"*): I said I told her, "Let me have it to hold, and to meditate . . . "

Charles: . . . I heard what you said.

John: So — then we needn't . . . there'll be money . . . let's not . . .

Charles: There'll be money when?

John: Soon.

Charles: And how will we "get" this money. (*Pause.*) How will this money *come* to us?

John (*pause*): It will come to us. At the *end*. When she *asks*, "How can I pay you?" We say, "Leave something. To help us with our work. Leave what you will . . . " They will ask and they will reward you. I told her to bring a photograph. Anything . . . Eh? This creates the habit. To bring something, to "bring" things to you . . . their thoughts . . . "money" . . . and when you don't *misuse* it, it creates confidence in them. And *when* we've helped her . . .

Charles: *When* we've *helped* her . . .

John: Yes. These things take time.

Charles (*simultaneously with "time"*): When we've helped her to *what*?

John: I've told you. To . . . to do whatever that is she wants to do. To . . . *face* herself . . . as we *will* help her . . . and she *will* reward us. And we're *making* progress. As you saw.

Charles: I saw.

John: Well, yes. You . . . you . . . she was won over. Didn't you see that?

Charles (*simultaneously with "see that"*): Perhaps.

John: Oh, no. SHE WAS WON OVER. She gave me the bill. She's going to bring the picture . . . slowly . . . slowly . . . you can't force the . . .

Coming to the Truth . . .

(*Pause.*) Don't you see that?

Charles (*simultaneously with "that"*): You said she dreamed this meeting.

John: . . . Ah. Did she forsee the meeting? We all dream of a wise man, one day . . . who will . . . I paint a picture. Looks like magic. You see her economic class . . . by the way: look at the shoes, anyone could buy a pricey dress . . . and we so we see an income of a certain magnitude. Suggests a summer house. Where? By the water is the obvious bet. And we suggest the mother nearby, you see? As the mother is the thing that draws her here. She's on her mind . . . and her mind . . . *freed* by "magic" . . .

Charles: . . . her mind freed by magic . . .

John: Yes. By my "clairvoyance." Yes. Yes. Yes. You must give them a *mechanism*. To allow them to *trust* you. She wouldn't trust just "anyone." She comes in: "Show me you have psychic powers." Alright. "Read my mind. Tell me my complaint." Alright. I will.

A troubled woman. Comes in. With a problem?
What is it? It's *money* — illness — *love* . . . That's all
it ever is. Money, illness or love.

A deeply repressed woman. In her thirties. Unmarried . . . as you say . . . Matter of the Heart? No.
Illness. Perhaps. Woman of an anxious nature, that
is a good bet. But no. I say "the fear of death." Three
times. And no reaction. In her eyes. And so. Health.
No. Love. No. And that leaves "money."

Charles: And you said "the Law."

John: I said a legal problem. How's this money come
to her, a wealthy woman, but there's *contracts* . . .
some legal . . .

Charles: You said "her mother's will."

John: Yes. I did.

Charles: How did you know that?

John: It was a guess. And an educated guess. Tech-
nique takes you so far, and then once in a while . . .

Charles: And that's all there . . . that's all there is.
(*Pause.*)

John: What?

Charles: That's all there is to what you do.

John: Well, I suppose we all want "magic," but our job, our *real* job . . .

One moment. I'm sorry . . . (*Pause.*) I'm sorry. You were speaking of money. I . . . I . . . what am I seeing . . . something came into my . . . evening . . . evening . . . eveningwear? A (*pause*) I see, what are they? Some stone? . . . Sapphire?

Charles: What is this?

John: Someone . . . a gift . . . they were *yours* . . . a set of sapphire studs. They . . . parted from them . . . ? You . . . no . . . yes. Valuable set of studs. A . . . a . . . and your concern with money and . . . you pawned a set of Sapphire Studs. (*Pause.*)

Charles: How do you know that?

John: Two weeks ago . . . before we met. Did . . . did you do that?

Charles: You . . . how could you know that?

John: I saw the pawn ticket. In your wallet. You see? Very simple, really. (*Pause.*) If one is allowed to believe . . . Our job is not to guess, but to *aid* . . . to . . . to create an atmosphere . . . As I just did with *you* . . . to enable . . .

Charles: What were you doing in my wallet?

John: Well. The man came with the *food*, I had to *tip* him . . . you were in the *shower*, I'm *sorry*. I did . . . I *certainly*

Charles: You should not have looked in my wallet.

John: No, you're absolutely right. I should . . . I should not. I'm sorry. I'm *very* sorry. Charles. I'm *very* sorry. I took a *dollar*, the ticket fell . . . you're absolutely right. And I apologize. (*Pause.*) I apologize. Will you forgive me? (*Pause.*) Will you please forgive me? (*Pause.*)

Charles: You're very nosy.

John: Yes, I. And I suppose that it's a professional . . . you're *right*. And I apologize. And I'm sorry as it's obvious that it's a touchy . . .

Charles: I should *say* that it's a "touchy." *Yes.* It. Well, I would say that it . . . .

John: We are going to have money. I *promise* you. When she comes to *us* asks *us*: "How can I repay you?" We say, "Leave what you will. To aid us in our work . . . Some would leave fifty, some would leave a thousand." . . . We are going to . . .

Charles: When?

John: Soon.

Charles: When?

John: As soon as I start to catch on. Which will be soon. Which, trust me, and she is the first sign, and a certain sign. I promise you. And we'll have your *studs* back, and . . .

Charles: . . . how long will it take?

John: However . . . a short while.

Charles: A short while.

John: Yes. (*Pause.*) And what I *have*. (*Pause.*) What I have . . . whatever I have, whatever I have is yours.

Charles: And just what is that now?

John: Just now that's very little. In material things. Very little. What I *can* offer you is: a . . . a profession. The beginnings of a craft. Which would sustain you, which . . .

Charles: A profession.

John: *Yes.* It *is.* To *help* . . . to . . . And I see what it is that *upsets* you. For the lack of money is a *sign* . . .

Charles: It is . . .

John: That something . . . yes, it is . . . that something *valuable* is missing. You have lost something which causes you to doubt. (*Pause.*) And I *see now* why it is you're disappointed. For your question is this: how legitimate is that thing which I do.

Charles: Is that my question?

John: Yes. It is. Though you don't *know* it is. That's why you balk at these . . . I *show* you the trick "from the back" and you're disappointed. Of course you are. If you view it as a "member of the audience." One of the, you will see, the most painful sides of the profession is this: you do your work well, and who will see it? No one, really . . . (*Pause.*) If you do it well. (*Pause.*) But . . . (*Pause.*) To say, to learn to say, I suppose you must, to just say what separates us, finally, from them is this: that is we look *clearly*. So be it. Not that we're "special" . . . (*Pause.*)

Charles: You told her that she was psychic.

John: . . . I tell that to everyone . . . Not that we're "mystic." But that we can see. Those very things which are before our eyes. Look at her. (*Pause.*) She is unmarried. At her time in life. Why? She is bound. To what? An unresolved event. Her mother's death? Her question, she would ask the "spirit world," her mother left a fortune to her stepfather. Should she contest this will in the courts. Is this a question for the mystic? No. It hides a deeper one: this: how can I face my betrayal. How can I obtain revenge. Against the dead. Or: why did my mother not love me more? And so we help her. To *answer* that *last* question.

Charles: And how is it we do that?

John: By telling her what she wants to know.

Charles: And what is that?

John: We don't know. We listen and she'll tell us . . . tomorrow. You'll listen again . . .

Charles: I will . . .

John: Yes.

Charles: And how many days will I listen?

John: How many . . . ?

Charles: What is this. A *month* . . . a *year*? How many . . .

John: I told you. . . . As we gain her *confidence*.

Charles: Her confidence. If it's a trade you should be paid for it.

John: We will.

Charles (*simultaneously with "will"*): You doing something for the girl or not? What are you frightened of . . . ? Should you be paid for this or not? Well *I* should. *I* should. Cause I'm sitting here, too.

(*Gets up.*) Where's the fifty.

John: Fifty.

Charles: Give me the bill.

John: I can't. How can I? She *signed* it. I have to give it back to her to . . .

Charles: What is this, a *child's* game? Give me the *bill.*

John: No, No, No. I *can't.* If she comes back here and the bill is gone . . .

I see. I see. Charles. Charles. I see. That . . . sit down, please. I see that I've humiliated you.

Charles: You have . . . ?

John: Over a "Dollar." Yes. For Nothing. For money. I went in your wallet. I see that you're *hurt* . . .

Charles: You see that . . .

John: Yes, and.

Charles: Well, you see it all. *Don't* you? Tell me what else do you see? You see that she wanted to contact the Spirits. (*Pause.*)

John: She, well, I *told* you that.

Charles: Now: what did she want you to do?

John: To throw a *seance*, to . . . you know, *effects* . . . miraculous . . . entities . . . unknown *facts* . . .

Charles: Unknown facts?

John: Facts only her mother could know.

Charles: And people could give those to her?

John: Of course.

Charles: How?

John: Uh, well, you just go to the library. Yearbooks. Society files . . . Research. You invent a "contact." Um. Some Spirit Medium. Lived in the Nineteenth Century. A friendly spirit gone before . . .

Charles: And you could do this?

John: I'm *telling* you. Once you have won their trust you . . .

Charles: You've *done* it?

John: No. I've *seen* it done. I've *seen* it done . . . What?

Charles: You know what?

John: No, no, that's why I asked you. What . . .
what . . . what . . .

Charles: We should use the tools that you've developed.

John: I do — use them. What do you . . . in what
way?

Charles: We should take her fortune from her.

John: Well, there are many who would.

Charles: Then we should do it.

John: Well. No. I don't think so. (*Pause*.) We all feel
greed . . . sometimes . . . for those things we cannot have, or which seem . . . things *myself*, things
that I want for *you*, for *us*, but if we just correctly
understand those . . .

Charles: You said that she wants a seance. And she's
going to have it. You said research. I want you to
tell me the research I should do. I'm going to do it.
When she comes tomorrow we'll give her her seance.
You'll make her mother suggest she should contest
the will and then give us the fortune.

John: No.

Charles: And you will *do* it or else I am leaving you. Do you understand?

(*Pause.*)

Do you understand me?

John: Would you force me to make that choice?

Charles: I've done it. Now the choice is yours.

Act Three

John, Charles and Miss A

John: Are you comfortable?

Miss A: Yes.

John: Would you . . . please remove your wrist-watch, your *rings* and loosen anything which constricts the free flow of blood. Charles:

Charles: Yes.

John: Dim the lights, please. (*Pause.*) Thank you. (*Pause.*) Now: are you ready to begin?

Miss A: Yes.

John: May we be *silent* a moment, and open our minds to that thing which we hope to do. Not to strain, not to *seek*, but simply to *open* ourselves. Quietly. Yes. (*Pause.*) We are here today to attempt to make *contact*. With one recently departed. Whose *soul* lingers here. Who *is* here with us . . . to attempt to *contact* her. To *ask* her: to address a question . . . and we seek the aid. Of someone gone before. (*Pause.*) To aid us. As they've aided us before. Yes, That's right. Are you alright?

Miss A: Yes. (*Pause.*)

John: The candles, please. SPIRITI MIEI INFER-
NALI OBEDITE. In the year eighteen forty-three
there lived in Boston a shopkeeper named Hawks.
Samuel Hawks. He kept a shop on Tremont Street.
Who sold tobacco, who dealt with all aspects of
society. A merchant captain who dealt with the
store, who supplied him, who bought from him, who
did business with Mr. Hawks and who was invited
to come to his home and who became a friend.
Many's the time he came there and he was welcomed
into the family; the captain came and told the stories
of the sea. Won over, he won over her, she was wooed
by his life and left her family to meet him. After-
noons by the docks, by the waterfront I went there
to his room he rented and it smelt of sweat, the curtains blowing on the dock, we saw the curtains blow,
the ship commands from down, men working men
on the wharves, do your bidding on the sea but what's
here? Used to native hands ways of the south which
we cannot imagine in extremity they make an offer
to their lord, some passion but the horror was he'd
brought it home. I was won to the danger he would
get away but how would I?

I would not. Immured in that house I prayed for
when he'd come, what can you ask but that I gave
it and he asked it and I did. I grabbed his hair and

helped him to me, I cried out what I discovered was that I had the disease, take me with you. No and so when he went . . . how could I say? Even my children here, who'd asked him to come, but he came, "you have ruined me." And Take Me. No. Take me upon your ship. No. No. How can you leave me in this room — clung to him threatened, his fierce, my mistake, threatened with the . . . you say that I reaped the desired result, that I won, stabbed, stabbed in the belly, ripped out with his dirk, bloodied the sheets, wiped it upon the wall, which, when he went out, not to the ship but back to the store, to take leave, to close the contract, when he'd killed me . . . told my husband he left his regards, while I was staring at it. His esteemed wife. Who, the tide set, standing at the helm. Felt no remorse. Felt nothing. Said nothing. All those years. Died respected. He died. When they would not claim my corpse. The voices from the wharf. I saw the Bloodmark, I, then he went in that room. I knew the afternoon before my husband brought him home. But seated there . . . (*Pause.*) And the servant said the race has bred the smell out of itself . . . and so was dying in its bed. Laid in disgrace. Lured to the squalid room and killed. Everyone knew. It seemed everyone knew but me. And so you come to me.

(*Pause.*)

As others have. And ask me. Hidden from all but not
from my pain.

I see a house. I see a white house.

(*Pause.*) I see a numeral.

Miss A: What do you see?

John: I see the number eight. A year . . . ?? I . . .
An address . . . ? I see the figure "eighty-four."

Miss A: Eighty-four. That . . .

John: What?

Miss A: That was our house on . . .

John (*simultaneously with "our"*): Why do you come
to me for help?

Miss A: That was our house on Rosemont Street . . .

John (*simultaneously with "Rosemont"*): A woman
has died, a dress, she . . . A *party* dress. White. Off-
white . . . rose . . . ?

Miss A: A . . .

John: A party dress. She gave you. That she bought . . . she bought it for you.

Miss A: She bought in Paris.

John: I see her there, and I . . . A night. What? You were, what?

Miss A: When she kissed me.

John: And I see her standing by your bed. She said. She said, "You are my . . . "

Miss A (*simultaneously with "my"*): "You are my little . . . "

John: I called to you.

Miss A: When?

John: I see her.

Miss A: What do you see?

John: I see her as she stood beside you. She is at your bed. A . . . a . . . a red brick building. She is in your room. She . . . at your door. A red brick building . . .

Miss A (*simultaneously with "building"*): That's my apartment . . .

John (*simultaneously with "apartment"*): She . . . you. Wait! You *felt* her there . . . last . . . last . . . *recently*. She *came* to you. She says . . .

Miss A: I . . .

John: "I *called* to you . . . " "Don't you *hear*??" When is this . . . ?

Miss A: It's . . . it's

John: When . . . when . . . ?

Miss A: It's my *apartment* . . .

John: She stood . . . don't you *hear* her? She stood by your bed. She *called* you. Are you . . . you asked, you prayed to her, to come, to reveal . . .

Miss A: What, I . . .

John: You hear a knocking. Your mother, "I called your name." But no faith. You *heard* her. She came to you, *say* it.

Miss A: I . . .

John: Your apartment. And you heard a knocking at the . . .

Miss A: I don't . . .

John: Yes! You *heard* her! The *wind* blew. SHE WAS CALLING YOUR NAME!!!

Miss A (*pause*): It was my name I thought . . .

John: You *know* it was. (*Pause.*) In your dream . . . she said, "What did you dream? And what did you dream that night?" And you told her your dream. "Sleep. For I am always with you." She said that to you. She called you. She *told* you. Oh. Those times. Those years. She mourned. How she mourned. How she . . . for your . . . for your grief, I've seen her. "My darling child . . . " Dreamt of the . . . stand, standing by the bed, called . . . "My darling child." And why do you resist me? And she said you have a question. Something troubles . . . ?

Miss A: The . . .

John: "I made a will . . . " The mon . . . the money . . . she left . . . she has left it. To . . . to someone *else*. She . . . She's saying . . . wait . . . I . . . (*Pause.*)

Charles: . . . go on . . .

John: I don't think I . . . I'm losing . . .

Charles: Go on.

Miss A: Will you please . . .

John: You have a photograph of her . . . ?

Miss A: I . . .

John: *Put* it. Face down on the table. "As, Alif Casyl, Zaza, Hit Mel Melat." Place your hands on it. (*Miss A does so.*) She . . .

(*Pause.*) I've . . .

I . . . (*Pause.*) You have a question . . . your dear mother . . . "Let this man decide." The question of . . . you're troubled . . . I . . . I . . . be assured she loves you . . . She says be free of the money. And you must forsake your . . . She: "I will never leave you." Your mother lives in you still. "Follow my counsel, and come again," and

Charles: . . . she says . . .

John (*simultaneously with "says"*): She loves you still. She . . . "I left you unwillingly . . . " And we will meet again . . . I'm . . . (*Pause.*) I'm . . . (*Pause.*) I see the shades, a mark upon the, she is in the room by the dock, I feel . . . (*Pause.*) I'm sorry. (*Pause.*)

Charles: Are you alright?

John: I'm fine. I . . . (*Pause.*) I'm fine. (*Pause.*) I need a second. What did I . . . ? Will you open the . . .

(*He gestures* Charles *to the windows, where the shades are opened.*)

(*Pause.*) (*Sighs.*) It's gone. (*Pause.*)

Miss A: And . . . ? (*Pause.*) May I speak . . . ?

John (*simultaneously with "speak"*): You want to . . . and the woman who spoke is that . . . ? What happened? (*Pause.*)

Charles: The Boston Woman.

John: Yes. The Boston Woman spoke. She . . . what did she . . . ? A concern for . . . she . . .

Charles: She said she made contact with the . . .

John (*to* Miss A): With your mother.

Miss A: Yes.

John: She said that?

Miss A: Yes.

John: And?

Miss A: She said, "Let the man decide."

John: Let . . . which means . . . ?

Miss A: To . . .

John: That *we* should decide. That *I* . . .

Miss A: Yes.

John: That I should decide about the legal . . .

Miss A: Yes.

John: I'm, I'm, I'm . . . That was the question you addressed to her . . . But not qualified, of course, I . . .

Miss A: You could . . .

John: I could what?

Miss A: Ad . . .

John: Advise . . . ?

Miss A: You could advise me. (*Pause.*)

John (*sighs*): No. I don't . . . I suppose I . . .

Miss A: You saw my mother. (*Pause.*)

John (*to* Miss A): The contact saw her. I retain a . . .
dimly . . . dimly . . .

Miss A: Was she as you see her in this photograph?

John: The photograph. Turn it up. (Miss A *does so.*)
Yes. Yes. She. Yes. (*Pause.*) She was somewhat *young-
er*. Your mother. As I saw her in . . .

Miss A (*simultaneously with "in"*): THAT'S NOT
HER PHOTOGRAPH. I TOOK IT FROM A BOOK.
You're all the, all of you, god *damn* you! How could
you, "I see her by the bed." How can you *prey* on
me? Is there no *mercy* in the world . . . ?

Charles: If you . . .

Miss A: If you can't *help* me, NO one can help me . . . why did I *come* here. All of you . . . Oh *God*, is there no . . . how can you *betray* me . . . You . . . you . . . God *damn* you . . . for "money" . . . ? God . . .

Charles: . . . get her out of here . . .

Miss A: May you rot in hell, in *prison*, in . . . you *charlatan*, you *thief* . . .

Charles: We've . . .

John: *No.* Oh God forgive me . . .

Miss A: If there's any power in the world . . . *(Rising.)*

John: No!

Miss A: . . . I'm going to . . .

John: Oh, God help me, I'm sorry . . .

Miss A: GET OUT OF MY WAY!

John: Oh, God Help Me. I see Your Sainted Mother.

Wrapped you in a Shawl. A Red Shawl . . . Which she brought back, which she wore, she whispered, "I Am Coming Home . . . " When she went out. Your father took her. For the evening. And. When she came home. Into your room, she draped it on the lamp. It cast a red . . .

Miss A: . . . No.

John: Yes. And she would sing to you, "Are you asleep? My lamb . . . ?" And she would sing, you hear her.

Miss A: No.

John: And she would cradle you. The shawl smelt of perfume. You lost it *when*? Five . . . Five . . .

Miss A: Yes.

John: What?

Miss A: Five years ago.

John: And told no one, and grieved, a yellow flower, a rose, in the middle, and a golden fringe, she sang, "Are you asleep my lamb?" And she thinks of you still. And calls to you. And she calls to you now. And I saw her by your bed. She Wore The Shawl.

Act Four

John and Charles

Charles: Well. (*Pause.*) I suppose . . . (*Pause.*) I suppose we . . . (*Pause.*) I'd like to *stay* here. (*Pause.*)

John: No. I . . . I . . . We've *done* that.

Charles: I said I'd like to stay here.

John: Yes. It cannot . . .

Charles: All you have to . . .

John: I wish it were so. It is not so, it is not all I . . .

Charles: What is it? You think you have to "atone"? You . . . ?

John: I . . . *I* . . . No, you see, that I . . . No. That's not it.

Charles: I Want To Know.

John: I'm sure you do.

Charles: I want . . .

John: The things we want. Many things that I want . . .

Charles: I want to stay with you.

John: And know the Question. "How will the World End." "Will I Be Rich."

Charles: Don't force me to go.

John: *Tricks.* Don't you . . . ? Attracted. So attracted . . . Ah . . . you want to know a trick. And when I show you a trick . . . "But you read her mind." (*Pause.*) Yes? I "suggested" her. That's all I did. Eh? And now you can feel superior. And there is no mystery. And then you can go. "The Secrets of the Pyramids?" No. I went to the library. Society files. Perhaps two pictures. Of a woman in a red-fringed shawl. Two different photos. Yes, a well-to-do woman. And what would one assume? She wore it often. She wore it out, and she wore it home. An anxious child, the child couldn't sleep. The mother wore it in the room. The child remembered it. Are you free now? Now that you know The Mysteries? (*Pause.*) The Pythagorean mysteries? (*Pause.*) The Sacred . . . ? (*Pause.*) Three cups. And which cup hides the ball . . . Well. No. You asked to . . . you . . . I have nothing to . . . I wish I . . . (*Pause.*) I . . . (*Pause.*) Are you content? (*Pause.*)

Charles: Am I content?

John: Will you . . . yes. Will you, you're now equipped to live in a world without mystery. And now you know all that I know. And now you may leave content. (*Pause.*)

Charles: Wait. You said, "a scar."

John: I . . . ?

Charles: You said, "a scar." The first time she came. A scar. On her left knee. She didn't know it *herself*.

John: A scar.

Charles: And she didn't know it herself. How could you?

John: One final mystery. She is right-handed. Now: as children we all fall. And, to break the fall a right-handed person falls on his left knee. Ninety percent of the right-handed people in the world have a small scar on their left knee. I'm sorry. (*Pause.*) Goodbye.

Charles: You said we all must learn.

John: Did I say that?

Charles: Yes. And . . . yes. And . . . you've *shown* me . . . and . . . wait! You said she lost it five years ago. How . . .

John: I TOLD YOU. IT WAS A *TRICK*. IT WAS A *TRICK*. ARE YOU *DEAF*? Live in the World. Will you, please? That's what *I'm* trying to do. I'd *wished* that we would be something more to each other. It was not to be.

Charles: I . . .

John: And so goodbye. I'm truly sorry to have disappointed you. (*Pause.*)

Charles: I . . . (*Pause.*) Goodbye.

John: Yes, we said that. (*Pause.* Charles *exits.* John *stands alone.*) "As, Alif Casyl, Zaza, Hitmel Meltat." (Miss A *enters.*) Yes, yes, yes. Come in. I . . . is it time already . . . ? for our . . . ?

Miss A: I'm a little early, may I . . . ?

John: Please.

Miss A: May I sit down?

John: Please.

Miss A: Thank you. (*Sits.*)

John: How are you today?

Miss A: I'm fine. I . . . are you alright?

John: Perfectly.

Miss A: . . . you seem . . . ?

John: I was with a client, and you are absolutely right. Now: let me clear my mind, and . . . (*Pause.*) Yes. Now. You seem . . . you've *decided* something, for you seem in better *spirits* today. Something has been . . . And a *burden* has been lifted from your mind. Good. I see *clarity*. Good. For there's so much sorrow in this life. A question answered. For, finally, we must solve them all in our own mind. And we know that is true. (*Pause.*) Good. (*Pause.*) Yes. Yes. What? What is it? (*Pause.*)

Miss A: I have to ask you something.

John: . . . but still skeptical. Good. We can't overcome our nature. For it protects us. You ask what you wish to ask.

Miss A: You won't be offended.

John: No. I promise you.

Miss A: If I were to . . . (*Pause.*)

John: Tell me. If you were to *what?*

Miss A: If I were to search in *Boston*. For a Mister Hawks.

John: Yes.

Miss A: And for his *wife*, in 1840 who was murdered . . .

John: If you search then what would you find? That it was a story, that someone made up. That it was true? Then someone could have read it. That it was not noted, then perhaps it had been overlooked.

Miss A: Mm.

John: I see that's insufficient, but it must suffice. You see: it's not *divination* that concerns you. Finally. The question of your mother's will. And I see you've decided.

Miss A: Yes. I'm going to contest the will.

John: I think that that is what you want to do.

Miss A: Yes. It *is*, it's exactly what I want to do (*Pause.*) And I'd like to *thank* you. (*Pause.*)

John: I'm glad to do what I can.

Miss A: And I'd like . . . how do I *pay* you?

John: You may pay me what you wish. And when you wish.

Miss A: . . . what is the usual . . . ?

John: Those, those that have been helped — some might, some, as they can afford it, as they wished, might pay up to a thousand dollars. To help us with our work. Some would leave fifty. Some would leave nothing. It's completely up to you. (*Pause.*)

Miss A: You made contact with my mother.

John: That is not the . . .

Miss A: You *contacted* her.

John: Well. Perhaps I did. And . . . I . . . I . . . I don't *know*.

Miss A: You saw her. No. You saw her wrap me in that shawl. No one could know that. You *saw* her.

John: *Did* I see her . . .

Miss A: No. You must *tell* me. (*Pause.*) You *must* tell me. You *saw* her. (*Pause.*)

John: Yes.

Miss A: You saw her wrap me in that shawl.

John: Yes. (*Pause.*)

Miss A: And you say I *lost* it.

John: You, yes, that is what I said. But you did *not* lose it. You *burnt* it. In rage. Standing somewhere by the water, five years ago.

Miss A: Yes. And then I . . . ?

John: I do not know. That is all I saw.

Prairie du Chien

Prairie du Chien was first produced by "Earplay" for National Public Radio in April 1979, with the following cast directed by Daniel Freudenberger: Charles Durning; Jeff Goldblum; Larry Block; and Bruno Kirby.

THE CHARACTERS

A Porter
A Card Dealer
A Gin Player
A Storyteller
A Listener
The Listener's Son

THE SCENE

The play takes place in a railroad parlor car heading west through Wisconsin in 1910. The time is three A.M.

Note: Directions in brackets pertain to radio production.

[*Sound: The continuous lulling sound of a railroad journey. We listen a while.*]

(*Note: All voices, except where indicated, should be very subdued, as suited to three a.m.*)

[*Sound: Cards being shuffled. Sound: Train whistling approaching a crossing. Long. Long. Short. Long.*]

Dealer: Cut.

Gin Player: I pass the cut.

Dealer: Right.

[*Sound: Cards being dealt.*]

One, one, Two, Two. Three and Three.

[*Sound: Dealer yawns.*]

Gin Player: You tired?

Dealer: No. And four and four. Five *five*, six *six*, and Seven *seven*, eight, *eight*, nine and *ten*.

Gin Player: Good.

· 57

Dealer: Three of diamonds. (*Yawns.*) He takes the three of diamonds.

[*Sound:* Porter *approaching.*]

(*Pause.*) And throws the king. (*Pause.*) Throws the cowboy.

Porter: Yassuh. Anything else I can get you gentlemen?

Dealer: No. Thank you.

Gin Player: No.

[*Sound: Money jingling.*]

Dealer: Here.

Porter: Thank you very *much* sir.

Dealer: Sure. Throws the K.

[*Sound:* Porter *retreating.*]

Gin Player: Play.

Dealer: Yah. (*Pause.*) I play the king right back.

(*Pause.*)And I get the *heart* five. (*Pause.*) The five of hearts. What does that tell us? (*Pause.*) When he has taken the three diamonds? (*Pause.*) When he has took the three of dimes?

[*Sound: The door to the car opens. Rushes of air, etc. The door is closed. Sound: We follow the footsteps of the person who has just come in. As he walks down the aisle the conversation of the card players fades.*]

Gin Player: It's your play.

Dealer: Yes. Alright. You use that? (*Pause.*) Eh? That's what I thought. And plays the ten.

[*Sound: The footsteps stop.*]

Storyteller (*expels air*): *Cold* out there! (*In an undertone.*)

Listener: I'll bet it is.

Storyteller: Phew! The boy still asleep?

Listener: Yep.

Storyteller: I wish I could sleep like that.

DAVID MAMET

Dealer (*in the background*): Jack.

Storyteller: 'Specially on a *long* ride.

Listener: Yes.

Storyteller: A *night* train. (*Pause.*) Never *could* sleep. (*Pause.*) *Never* sleep. Where was I?

Dealer: Take it.

Listener: Up in Council Bluffs, I think.

Storyteller: That's right. Now I was *telling* you I'm up in Council Bluffs.

Dealer: The six of diamonds. Six of diamonds and the five of hearts. Go on and take it. Take it, 'cause you *know* you want it.

Gin Player: Well, I don't know if I want it yet, or not.

Storyteller: . . . And this man owned a *drygoods* store. I'd see him five, six times a year when I'd swing through. Eh? Always good for a small order. Nothing great. But steady.

Listener: Right.

Storyteller: He had a lovely little wife.

Listener: A young man.

Storyteller: In his fifties.

Listener: Uh-huh.

Storyteller: In his fifties. (*Pause.*) And married two years at the time, perhaps. At that time that I speak of. (*Pause.*) He had a small farm out of town.

Listener: Yes.

Storyteller (*pause*): He might have *been* something back East. But I don't know exactly. No one knew. Not even afterwards.

Dealer: Four.

Gin Player: You're going down with four?

Dealer: Yes. Yes. I think I am.

Storyteller: And his wife?

Listener: Yes?

Storyteller: My *God* she was a pretty thing.

Listener: Mmm.

Storyteller: And he was a jealous man. A very jealous man. Of money, too. Very tight-fisted. Always thought that he was being cheated. I can tell you. Smart, though. (*Pause.*) A clever man. (*Pause.*) There was talk he'd been a lawyer in the East.

Listener: Mmm.

Storyteller: And he was always bitter. As if he'd come *down*, you know? (*Pause.*) As if he'd come *down*, in life. (*Pause.*) Very bitter. *She* was kind, though. (*Pause.*) To me. A lovely woman. (*Pause.*) When I'd come through. If she was in the store. They lived out on the farm. I told you?

Listener: Yes.

Storyteller: Just out of town. Him and their hand and her. (*Pause.*) And she was just not happy. When I saw her. As the months went by. I saw her fade. (*Pause.*)

[*Sound: The slap of cards.*]

(*The Storyteller sighs.*) And then one time when I came in. (*Pause.*) And this is what I told you. (*Pause.*) I saw the welts.

[*Sound: From the back of the car we hear low whistling: "The Banks Of The Wabash."*]*

(*Pause.*) I saw bruises on her face and hands.

Listener: Mmm.

Storyteller: I had just come in. One day in March. She came up to the store. She had been driven by their hand. This colored man. He stayed down in the wagon and she came inside.

Listener: When was this?

Storyteller: Spring. March. Sometimes warm. Disturbing. Wet. One day cold, this one warm. I could see she was disturbed. She drew him in the corner. They had you know, they had words. He turned to me: "What are you looking at?" he says. And there was *hate* in his eyes . . . ?

*See special note on copyright page.

DAVID MAMET

Listener: Mmm.

Storyteller: I mean to tell you. (*Pause.*) And then he took to ask me when I'd come in, had I seen his *wife*. (*Pause.*) Had I seen her on the street . . . in any other town. . . . He said: "I worry when I'm not at home," his eyes, he had this tone, sarcastic, and you never knew if he was serious or what. (*Pause. Mimicking.*) "Have you seen my *wife*?" In town they told me he would check the buggy horses in the evening when he got home to see were they *tired*. (*Pause.*) If they'd been *out*.

Listener: Why didn't he ask the hired man?

Storyteller: He didn't trust him. Not by this time. Not at all.

Dealer (*faintly*): You know you want it.

Storyteller: No. (*Pause.*) He was sure that she was stepping out on him. He had seen, he said that he had seen (*Sotto.*) Is the boy asleep?

Listener: Yes.

Storyteller: *Traces* . . . (*Pause.*) Eh?

Listener: Yes.

Storyteller: And he knew that she had been unfaithful. (*Pause.*)

Dealer: You know you want it. Soo-cide jacks, Man with the Ax. Go on and take it.

Storyteller: He knew she was stepping out. I'll tell you: one day my route brought me back. When I was swinging back I come in to the store. He has a *grin* on his face? (*Pause.*) Such a strange grin.

Listener: Mmm.

Storyteller: Not healthy. Not at all. In August. (*Pause.*) Dust in the air. (*Pause.*) Murder in the air. (*Pause.*) You could feel it. Animals could feel it. (*Pause.*) I tried to pass the time of day with him. He couldn't hear a word I said. "What is it, friend?" I said. "What's on your mind?" "I'm going to kill my wife," he says.

Dealer: He takes the four.

Storyteller: "I'll tell you," he says. "If you ask. She's going to have a child. It isn't mine. And I am going to kill her." (*Pause.*) "She's going to tell me who the father is, and then I'll kill her." Well. (*Pause.*) I tried talking to the man. I tried to keep him there. But he would not be held. We struggled. I don't think it was a contest. He was full of strength from hate. He hit me with something. He knocked me down. (*Pause.*) When I got up he was gone. (*Pause.*) I went for the sheriff.

[*Sound: Whistling stops.*]

Listener: Were you hurt?

Storyteller: I was not hurt. No. No. I found the sheriff. And I told him. Just what I told *you.* We rode out to the farm. From on a crest, about a half a mile out we saw a glow. The farm was burning. In the dusk. The barn was burning. We rode to the house. What did we see? (*Pause.*) On the porch. The farmer. Hanging from the crossbeam. Dead. His shotgun on the ground.

Listener: He hung himself?

Storyteller: Wait. And we heard. What sounded like a woman crying. In the house. (*Pause.*) Softly crying. Softly. (*Pause.*) The sheriff went inside. (*Pause.*) Cautiously. I waited on the porch. (*Pause.*) I heard voices. (*Pause.*) I heard, it sounded like: "Go to the barn." A woman's voice. "Go to the barn. Please. Help him."

Gin Player: Twelve.

Dealer: And three from twelve is nine.

Storyteller: So I went to the barn. (*Pause.*) Burning. Burning. Through the doorway I could see the hired man. (*Pause.*) He was dead. (*Pause.*) Lying in the middle of the barn. He had a harness in his hand, and he had had a pitchfork stuck right up beneath his heart. (*Pause.*) And he'd been cut. His overalls were ripped down and the man had cut him. (*Pause.*) It was sickening. Five feet away there was the woman. In this lovely dress. This red dress. On her face. Her back was blowed away. And both of 'em are dead. (*Pause.*) And the barn's about to go.

Dealer: You want it? Do you want the card?

Gin Player: Yes.

Storyteller: And the barn's about to go. (*Pause.*) Well, I start back to the house. Eh? On the way I meet the sheriff coming down. He says, "Come on." "The nigger's in the barn." "I know," I say. "He's dead." "You sure he's dead?" the sheriff says. "Yes," I say. "Yes. I'm sure. Her, too. The both of 'em are dead." "Who?" he says. "Both of who?" "Him and the wife. The hand and her. He's killed 'em both." "No." (*Pause.*) He says. "Don't tell me that she's dead. Don't tell me that she's dead when I just saw her in the house." "Saw who?" "The wife. Mrs. McGurney," he says.

"In the house. She told me to come down here. (*Pause.*) She told me to look in the barn." "Well, someone's dead," I say. "Him and a woman. Some white woman." We run to the barn. And he is talking to himself. He's mumbling, "She told me to come *down* here. No. To help the nigger." (*Pause.*) We get there, barn's about to go now, any second. Cinders in the air as big as your hand. We stood in the door. The sheriff shouts "Hallo!" The smoke blows. There they are. The two of them. (*Pause.*) In the middle of the barn. He's on his back. And she, I don't know, she has *crawled* to him. I would have sworn that she was dead. (*Pause.*) She has *moved* to him, and she has got her head upon his chest. "That's her!" he says. "That's her!" "That's *who*?" (*Pause.*) I said. "Who?" And then the barn caved in.

Gin Player: Porter!

[*Sound:* Porter *approaches.*]

Porter: Yassuh?

Gin Player: What time is it?

Porter: Two fifty-three, sir.

Gin Player: Thank you.

[*Sound:* Porter *retreats.*]

Storyteller: "That's who?" I said. "Mrs. McGurney."

Dealer: Okay, then. That's sixty that you owe me, sixty, sixty-two, we'll call it sixty.

Gin Player: Thank you.

[*Sound: Humming "Redwing."*]*

Storyteller: "Now wait," I say. "Wait. Didn't you just say you saw her in the *house?*" (*Pause.*) There was something in the air then. (*Pause.*) As if the air got thick. The barn was so hot. We fell back. The sheriff's shaking. He started to walk. To go back to the house. There was a smell like, I don't know. Like sweat. Like sick sweat. Do you know? We went back. (*Pause.*) And we went in. And all the time he mumbled to himself. "No. No." (*Pause.*) Very softly. We went in. And room by room we searched the house. We started in the cellar. There was no one there. (*Pause.*) There was no one there. In the whole house. (*Pause.*) We searched every room. Up to the attic. (*Listener makes a shivering sound.*) He'd seen her. (*Pause.*) He said he'd seen her. I heard some-

*See special note on copyright page.

thing. (*Pause.*) And I would swear to that. But he said that he'd seen the woman. There was nothing in the house. Until as we were coming down the attic stairs. "Look. Look!" he said. Then I saw something. To this day I could not tell you what it was. A form. (*Pause.*) Something blowing. I don't know. "It's *her*!" he says. It went into the bedroom. Something went. I don't know. (*Pause.*) The door slammed. (*Pause.*)

Dealer: You deal.

Gin Player: *High* card deals.

Dealer: I'm sorry. You are absolutely right.

[*Sound:* Porter *enunciates first line of chorus softly:* "Now the Moon shines tonight on Little Redwing . . . " *continues humming.*]

Storyteller: We went in. Through the bedroom door. (*Pause.*) We opened the bedroom door. (*Pause.*) There was no one in the room. The window was down and locked. (*Pause.*) There was only one door in the room besides the one we came in through. And it went to the closet.

Dealer: Nine and nine and ten and ten and three of diamonds.

Storyteller: And we stood there. (*Pause.*) He cocked his gun. (*Pause.*) And he motioned me to stand to one side. (*Pause.*) Well, my friend, I began to pray.

Gin Player: Five.

Storyteller: He moved to pull the closet door back. Then the door *behind* us was flung open. Well, we spun around. There were these three men from the town. (*Pause.*) Gaping at us. "Get out!" they said. "Get out cause she's coming down!" The house had caught a cinder from the barn. "Get out!" they said. "She's burning!" "No, I'm *coming* out," he says. "I'm *coming* out. I'm checking." "Well, you *best* get out," they said. And they went. We could hear them going through the house. "Haloooo! Is anybody there?" (*Pause.*) "Is anybody here?" He locked the door. He locked us in the room. He looked at me, and then he locked us in the room. And he stared at the closet. I heard something. I think that I heard something. It could have been the wind. (*Pause.*) It could be crying. Softly crying. In the closet. (*Pause.*) He grasped the handle, and he threw it open. There was no one there. (*Pause.*) It was empty. Except for this dress. This pretty red dress. (*Pause.*) And it was burning. (*Pause.*) The hem was burning. All around. As if that it had just been lit. The flames were rising. "For the love of God, let's leave here," I said. "Please." "Oh *no!"* (*Pause.*) He was moaning to himself. "No!" The room was full of smoke. I had to drag him from the closet door. "Come on, man. For God's *sake* come on . . . !" (*Pause.*) I met the townsmen on the stairs. "You have to help me," I said. "He's had too much smoke." We dragged him from the house. The house was burning down, the barn was gone. (*Pause.*) The two bodies still inside. We watched the rafters fall. The night was gray. It was a strange, gray color, and the air was full of smells. We left the sheriff by the house. When we came back he was asleep. We woke him up. We all were going back to town. (*Pause.*) There was going to be an autopsy.

Listener: On the storekeeper.

Storyteller: On him, yes. He was the only one. We all gave depositions at the courthouse. This is what he said. "I have been sleeping." This is what the sheriff said. "I have been sleeping. We rode out there. He was hanging. They were dead inside the barn." And then he went to sleep. (*Pause.*) In the courthouse. (*Pause.*) He could not stay awake.

Dealer: Twelve.

Gin Player: And twenty's thirty-two.

Storyteller: He could not stay awake. And they

thought he was ill. But there was nothing wrong with him.

Gin Player: Deal.

Storyteller: Three years later he was killed.

Listener: The sheriff.

Storyteller: From the night the barn burned he was never right. They told me. When I came through. (*Pause.*) *Never* right. He slept the whole time. (*Pause.*) His wife deserted him. (*Pause.*) He lost his job, of course.

Listener: Yes.

Storyteller: He was not well. (*Pause.*) And then this man caught him. There had been *stories* . . . Is the boy asleep?

Listener: Yes. (*Pause.*)

Storyteller: There had (*whispering*) been those *stories* . . . and then this man caught him with his daughter.

Listener: Caught the sheriff with his daughter.

Storyteller: Yuh.

Listener: How old was she? (*Pause.*)

Storyteller: Ten. (*Pause.*) Ten years old.

Listener: No!

[*Sound: Train approaches crossing and whistle hoots. Long, long short long.*]

Storyteller: Yes. He told him, listen to this: "I am going to take my daughter home. You tell me where you're going to be. Because I have to talk to you." The sheriff told him he would be at home. (*Pause.*) Eh?

Listener: Yes.

Storyteller: Ten years old. (*Pause.*) And the man went to his house. He went in. He called. This is what I'm told. (*Pause.*) There was no one there. (*Pause.*) He heard someone rocking. On the floor above. (*Pause.*) Rocking in a chair. He heard the squeaking. He went up. He threw the door back and there was the sheriff. In a rocking chair.

Dealer: He takes the jack, he doesn't take the ten.

Storyteller: There is the sheriff dressed in a red dress. (*Pause.*) A red gingham dress. (*Pause.*) Rocking. (*Pause.*) He said, "Please help him. They are in the barn. (*Pause.*) Help him. Please." (*Pause.*)

Dealer: Eight.

Storyteller: "Please help him."

Gin Player: You call with *eight*? The hell you say! (*Pause.*) Lay them down. Just lay them down and let's see what you've got.

Storyteller: In a red gingham dress. (*Pause.*) "Help him. Help him. Please."

Dealer: Here, count 'em up yourself.

Gin Player: I will, yes thank you.

Dealer: Have you had enough?

Gin Player: What? No.

Storyteller: Dressed like a lady. Eh? And rocking back and forth.

Listener: What happened to the animals?

DAVID MAMET

Gin Player: Cut for the deal.

Storyteller: What animals?

Dealer: Six.

Gin Player: Four.

Dealer: Six deals.

Listener: The *animals*. (*Pause*.) In the barn.

Storyteller: *McGurney's* barn.

Listener: Yes.

Storyteller: What about them? You mean when the *barn* burned.

Listener: Yes. (*Pause*.)

Storyteller: What about them.

Listener: Were they in the barn.

Dealer: Six *six*, and seven *seven*, eight and eight . . .

Storyteller: Yes.

Dealer: Nine and ten and king of clubs.

Listener: Why didn't they die? (*Pause.*)

Storyteller: Well, I guess they *did*. (*Pause.*) I guess that they *did*. (*Pause.*) I guess that they *did*.

Dealer: He takes the three of clubs.

Storyteller: The horses and the cows . . .

Gin Player: May I please see your cards?

Storyteller (*to himself*): All dead . . .

Dealer: I'm sorry . . . ?

Gin Player: May I see your cards?

Dealer: You want to see my cards.

Gin Player: Yes.

Storyteller (*to himself*): Yep, yep, yep, yep, yep.

Dealer: Why do you want to see my cards?

Gin Player: Just put 'em down.

DAVID MAMET

[*Sound: Way back in the car the* Porter *has started humming to himself "Meet Me In St. Louis."*]*

Dealer: I . . . wait. I want to tell you something.

Gin Player: Lay your cards down.

Dealer: I've got ten cards in my hand, friend. Same as you.

Gin Player: I'm asking nicely. (*Pause.*) I want to see your hand.

Dealer: And what if I don't want to show it to you? (*Pause.*) I'm not cheating you, friend. (*Pause.*) I'm not cheating you.

Gin Player (*raising his voice*): Count your cards. Just lay 'em down and count 'em.

Dealer (*pause*): Alright. One. Two. Three. Four, five, six. (*Pause.*) Seven. (*Pause.*) Eight. (*Pause.*) Nine, ten. Eh? Are you satisfied. You owe me eighty-seven dollars. (*Pause.*) It's time to settle up.

Gin Player: I want to play some more.

*See special note on copyright page.

Dealer: You do?

Gin Player (*pause*): Yes.

Dealer (*pause*): Alright.

Storyteller: So where you folks coming from?

Listener: Chicago.

Storyteller: Mmm. (*Pause.*) Where you going to?

Listener: Duluth.

Storyteller: The boy in school?

Listener: Yes.

Storyteller: Mmm. (*Pause.*) Fine-looking boy.

Dealer: Cut for the deal.

Storyteller: Up to Duluth, eh?

Listener: Yes.

Gin Player: Five.

Dealer: A doctor. King of hearts. I deal.

[*Sound: Sound of train changes slightly.*]

Porter (*to himself*): We coming down the hill for water. Five minutes we be crost the bridge. I always tell it by the soun'.

Dealer: And two and two and three and three. (*Pause.*) Four, four, five, five, the six and six and seven, seven, eight, eight, nine and ten. (*Pause.*) Two of spades.

Gin Player: Pass.

Dealer: I pass, too.

Storyteller (*to himself*): The skirt in flames around her ankles.

Dealer: Two.

Gin Player: Two. I take it.

Storyteller: . . . From the hem.

Dealer: Three.

Storyteller: . . . Lapping up. As if that it had just been lighted.

Dealer: Four. He drops the three, he drops the four.

Gin Player: Just play.

Storyteller: And sleeping with the hired man.

Dealer: A stranger. Queen of clubs.

Storyteller: . . . The boy asleep?

Dealer: The queen of clubs.

Listener: Yes . . .

Storyteller: Heavy with his child. (*Pause.*) They say.

Dealer: Takes the queen.

Storyteller: You can't know. Many things. You travel on a route up here.

Dealer: He takes it.

Storyteller (*to himself*): *Many* things.

Dealer: He takes the queen and throws the ten.

Storyteller: They think that they can talk to you, 'cause they see you so seldom.

DAVID MAMET

Porter (*to himself*): Slowin' down.

Gin Player (*yelling*): You son of a bitch! You're crimping *cards* on me! Don't touch that hand!

Dealer: Now, wait. Now look: Look, we'll just throw it in. Just pay me what you owe me and let's quit. Alright. Look, we'll just throw it in . . .

Gin Player: Don't you touch those cards you . . .

[*Sound: A pistol is fired twice.*]

Porter: Oh, my sweet Jesus!

Boy: Poppa!

Listener (*sotto*): Don't move. (*Pause.*)

Gin Player: Did I hit you?

Dealer: Oh, my God . . .

Storyteller: Whyn't you give me that gun, mister. Whyn't you just hand it to me . . . ?

Gin Player: Did I hit you? (*Pause.*)

Storyteller: Why don't you give me the gun?

82 ·

Gin Player: Did I hit you?

Dealer: No.

Storyteller: Give me the gun. That's good. Give me the gun. Good. (*Pause.*)

Listener: Did he hit the man?

Storyteller: No. Now you sit down. Just sit down. Good, now.

Boy: Poppa . . . ?

Listener: It's alright.

Boy: What happened?

Listener: Nothing. These men had a fight. (*Pause.*) It's alright. Go back to sleep. (*Pause.*) Everything's alright now.

Boy: Where are we?

Listener: You go to sleep. We have a long long time to go yet.

Gin Player: He. (*Pause.*) He was cheating me.

Dealer: No one was cheating you. You're *crazy*, friend. (*Pause.*) Eh? You're *crazy*, fellow.

Gin Player: He was crimping cards.

Dealer: Where? Where? Show me one card. Show me one card marked. (*Pause.*) Eh? You son of a bitch. They ought to lock you up. They ought to take a *strap* to you. (*Pause.*) If you can't lose, don't *play*.

Gin Player (*pause*): I'm sorry.

Dealer: Well, you owe me eighty-seven dollars here. (*Pause.*)

Gin Player: Yes. Yes.

[*Sound: Train whistles. Sound: Train begins to slow down.*]

Here. Yes. Thank you.

[*Sound: Porter walking through car.*]

Porter: Water stop. This. Prairie du Chien. Just about five minutes. Anybody want to stretch they legs we taking on some water.

[*Sound: Train whistle.*]

Gin Player: Eighty. Eighty-five. Six. Seven.

[*Sound: Train coming to a stop. Blowing off of steam.*]

I'm sorry.

Porter: Prairie du Chien.

Dealer: Get me my bag, eh?

Porter: Yassuh.

[*Sound: Bag being taken from rack. Panting. Sound: Progress of* Porter *and* Dealer *walking through car with bags.*]

Porter: I got it, you just watch your step, suh, getting down. (*Pause. We listen to the sounds of the train taking on water, cooling, etc.*)

Storyteller: Well! (*Pause.*) Well, I think that I'll step down and get some air. (*Pause.*) Join me?

Listener (*softly*): Son? (*Pause.*) Son? (*Pause.*)

Storyteller: Is that boy asleep again?

Listener: Son?

Storyteller: Can you beat that? (*Pause.*) I'd give a lot to sleep like that. (*Pause.*) Yes, I would. Yessir, I would.

[*Sound: We listen to the sound of the train for a moment.*]